Tools Search Notes Discuss MyReportLinks.com Books Go!

STATES

MASSACHUSETTS

A MyReportLinks.com Book

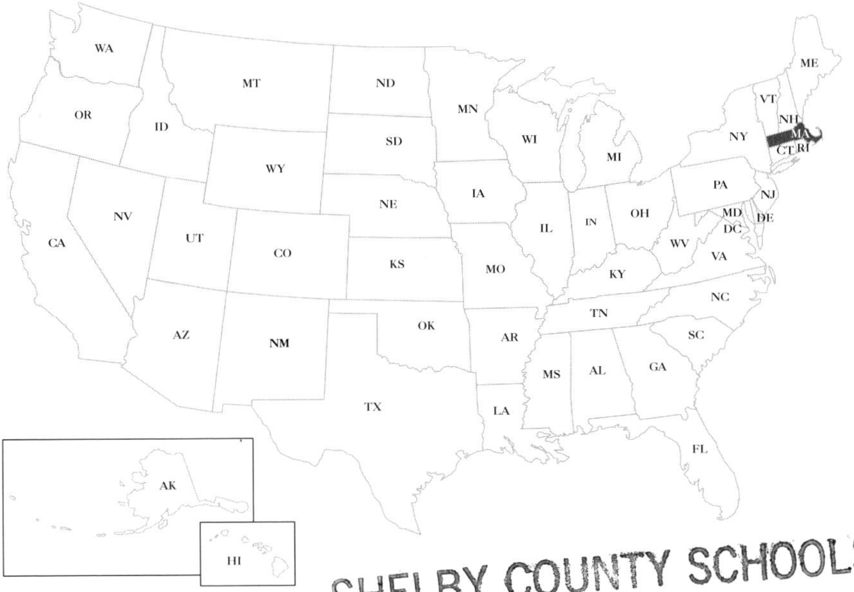

Corinne J. Naden & Rose Blue

MyReportLinks.com Books
an imprint of
Enslow Publishers, Inc.
Box 398, 40 Industrial Road
Berkeley Heights, NJ 07922
USA

MyReportLinks.com Books, an imprint of Enslow Publishers, Inc. MyReportLinks is
a trademark of Enslow Publishers, Inc.

Library of Congress Cataloging-in-Publication Data

Naden, Corinne J.
    Massachusetts / Corinne J. Naden & Rose Blue.
        p. cm. — (States)
        Summary: Discusses the land and climate, economy, government, and
history of the state of Massachusetts. Includes Internet links to Web sites.
    Includes bibliographical references and index.
    ISBN 0-7660-5107-2
    1. Massachusetts—Juvenile literature. [1. Massachusetts.]
I. Blue,Rose. II. Title. III. States (Series : Berkeley Heights, N.J.)
F64.3 .N33 2003
974.4—dc21
                            2002003416

Printed in the United States of America

10 9 8 7 6 5 4 3 2 1

To Our Readers:
Through the purchase of this book, you and your library gain access to the Report Links that specifically back
up this book.
The Publisher will provide access to the Report Links that back up this book and will keep these Report Links
up to date on **www.myreportlinks.com** for three years from the book's first publication date.
We have done our best to make sure all Internet addresses in this book were active and appropriate when we
went to press. However, the author and the Publisher have no control over, and assume no liability for, the
material available on those Internet sites or on other Web sites they may link to.
The usage of the MyReportLinks.com Books Web site is subject to the terms and conditions stated on the
Usage Policy Statement on **www.myreportlinks.com**.
In the future, a password may be required to access the Report Links that back up this book. The password
is found on the bottom of page 4 of this book.
Any comments or suggestions can be sent by e-mail to comments@myreportlinks.com or to the address on
the back cover.

Contents

MyReportLinks.com Books
Great Books, Great Links, Great for Research!

MyReportLinks.com Books present the information you need to learn about your report subject. In addition, they show you where to go on the Internet for more information. The pre-evaluated Report Links that back up this book are kept up to date on **www.myreportlinks.com**. With the purchase of a MyReportLinks.com Books title, you and your library gain access to the Report Links that specifically back up that book. The Report Links save hours of research time and link to dozens—even hundreds—of Web sites, source documents, and photos related to your report topic.

Please see "To Our Readers" on the Copyright page for important information about this book, the MyReportLinks.com Books Web site, and the Report Links that back up this book.

Access:

The Publisher will provide access to the Report Links that back up this book and will try to keep these Report Links up to date on our Web site for three years from the book's first publication date. Please enter **SMA5816** if asked for a password.

Report Links

The Internet sites described below can be accessed at
http://www.myreportlinks.com

▶**The Massachusetts Historical Society**   *EDITOR'S CHOICE

At the Massachusetts Historical Society Web site you will find
information about John Quincy Adams, Abigail Adams, Paul Revere,
Harriet Beecher Stowe, and other important historical figures.

Link to this Internet site from http://www.myreportlinks.com

▶**Explore the States: Massachusetts**   *EDITOR'S CHOICE

America's Story from America's Library, a Library of Congress Web site,
provides information about the state of Massachusetts. Here you will
find basic facts and interesting stories about the state.

Link to this Internet site from http://www.myreportlinks.com

▶**Boston History and Architecture**   *EDITOR'S CHOICE

This comprehensive Web site provides detailed information about
Boston's architecture, statues, places, and historic people and events.
Learn about Fenway Park, how Boston got its name, and much more.

Link to this Internet site from http://www.myreportlinks.com

▶**Interactive State House**   *EDITOR'S CHOICE

At this Massachusetts sponsored web site, readers will find a collection of
online resources and official fun facts. Nicknamed the Bay State, students
will discover its other nicknames, along with the state's official dog, cat,
insect, cookie, flower, dessert, fossil, song, beverage and much more.

Link to this Internet site from http://www.myreportlinks.com

▶**Commonwealth of Massachusetts: We'd Love to**   *EDITOR'S CHOICE
Show you Around

This Web site provides basic facts about the state of Massachusetts.
Here you will find links to presidential birthplaces, government
information, climate, and much more.

Link to this Internet site from http://www.myreportlinks.com

▶**Natureworks: Massachusetts Resources**   *EDITOR'S CHOICE

At this Web site you will find resources to Massachusetts State parks,
aquariums, botanical gardens, museums, zoos, and much more. You
will also find links to national parks such as Boston Harbor Island and
Cape Cod National Sea Shore.

Link to this Internet site from http://www.myreportlinks.com

 The Internet sites described below can be accessed at
http://www.myreportlinks.com

▶ Adams Papers

At this Web site you will find a collection of documents related to former United States President John Adams. Read letters written by Adams to George Washington and letters regarding the Declaration of Independence. You will also find a time line and biographical sketches.

Link to this Internet site from http://www.myreportlinks.com

▶ An Evening at Pops

At this PBS Web site you will learn about Symphony Hall located in Boston, Massachusetts. Symphony Hall is known as one of the great concert halls and at this Web site you will learn why.

Link to this Internet site from http://www.myreportlinks.com

▶ Anne Marbury Hutchinson

At this Library of Congress Web site, you will learn about Anne Hutchinson, America's first religious leader.

Link to this Internet site from http://www.myreportlinks.com

▶ Boston Massacre: March 5, 1770

America's Story from America's Library, a Library of Congress Web site tells the story of the Boston Massacre. Here you learn about the building conflict between American colonists and the British Royal Army, which resulted in the Boston Massacre.

Link to this Internet site from http://www.myreportlinks.com

▶ A Chronological History of New Bedford

This Web site provides a comprehensive history of New Bedford, Massachusetts. Here you will learn about New Bedford's history from 1602 to 1995. You will also find information about geography, the environment, history, and culture.

Link to this Internet site from http://www.myreportlinks.com

▶ The *Constitution*

At this PBS Web site you will find an overview of the USS *Constitution*, the oldest commissioned vessel in the United States Navy. You will also learn about Paul Revere's connection to "Old Ironsides."

Link to this Internet site from http://www.myreportlinks.com

Report Links

The Internet sites described below can be accessed at http://www.myreportlinks.com

▶ **Cranberries.org**

The official Cape Cod Cranberry Growers Association Web site describes the origin and history of cranberries, contains Cran-Facts, and there is a harvest festival calendar. You will also learn the importance of the cranberry industry to the state's economy.

Link to this Internet site from http://www.myreportlinks.com

▶ **The Emily Dickinson International Society**

The Emily Dickinson International Society Web site provides information about this famous writer, including photographs, biographical resources, and links to Dickinson's poems and letters.

Link to this Internet site from http://www.myreportlinks.com

▶ **Herman Melville's Arrowhead**

At this Web site you can visit Arrowhead, home of Herman Melville in Pittsfield, Massachusetts. Here you will learn about Melville's family history and connection to Berkshire County.

Link to this Internet site from http://www.myreportlinks.com

▶ **John Fitzgerald Kennedy Library and Museum**

At the John Fitzgerald Kennedy Library and Museum, in Boston, Massachusetts, you will find biographies, speeches, photographs, and other helpful resources.

Link to this Internet site from http://www.myreportlinks.com

▶ **Liberty! The American Revolution**

This PBS Web site provides an online companion to "LIBERTY! The American Revolution." This Web site features images, time lines, war highlights, a game, and much more.

Link to this Internet site from http://www.myreportlinks.com

▶ **Mass.gov**

The official Massachusetts Web site provides links to information about Massachusetts' government, elected officials, businesses, tourism, and much more.

Link to this Internet site from http://www.myreportlinks.com

 The Internet sites described below can be accessed at
http://www.myreportlinks.com

▶**Massachusetts Audubon Society**
At the Massachusetts Audubon Society Web site you will learn about conservation efforts in Massachusetts, sanctuaries, and birds. You will also find a section just for kids that teaches all about interesting creatures.

Link to this Internet site from http://www.myreportlinks.com

▶**Massachusetts Lights**
Visit the Boston Lighthouse Web site where you will learn about the history of lighthouses and find detailed descriptions of several lighthouses located in Massachusetts including Chatham, Cape Cod, Martha's Vineyard, Nantucket, and Gloucester.

Link to this Internet site from http://www.myreportlinks.com

▶**Massachusetts Maple Producers Association**
The Massachusetts Maple Producers Association is a fun-filled Web site. It covers just about anything and everything that has to do with maple sugaring—the history of maple syrup, how to make your own, and even maps of sugar house locations.

Link to this Internet site from http://www.myreportlinks.com

▶**The Mayflower Society**
The Mayflower Society Web site provides a brief history of the Mayflower pilgrims. You can also take a tour of the Mayflower House museum and read the Mayflower Compact of 1620.

Link to this Internet site from http://www.myreportlinks.com

▶**The Norman Rockwell Museum at Stockbridge**
Although Norman Rockwell was born in New York City in 1894, he later made Stockbridge, Massachusetts, his home in 1953. Rockwell received the nation's highest civilian honor, the Presidential Medal of Freedom, for his profound and brilliant interpretations of life in America.

Link to this Internet site from http://www.myreportlinks.com

▶**The Official Site of the Boston Red Sox**
When you just cannot get enough baseball, turn to the Boston Red Sox's official Web site. Here you will find baseball news, scorecards, an event schedule, baseball basics, an official club site, baseball tips from professionals, and loads of photographs.

Link to this Internet site from http://www.myreportlinks.com

Report Links

The Internet sites described below can be accessed at
http://www.myreportlinks.com

▶**Religion and the Founding of the American Republic**
At this Web site you can explore the history of religion in early
America. Learn about religious refuges, religion and the American
Revolution, and religion and the government.

Link to this Internet site from http://www.myreportlinks.com

▶**Salem Witch Museum 1692**
Walk through the Doors of the Salem Witch Museum and discover the
facts about Salem Witch Trials of 1692 and learn why nineteen people
were accused of practicing witchcraft and what became of them.

Link to this Internet site from http://www.myreportlinks.com

▶**Spy Letters of the American Revolution, From the
Collections of the Clements Library**
The Spy Letters of the American Revolution Web site provides primary
sources, time lines, and other interesting information regarding how
spies affected the American Revolution.

Link to this Internet site from http://www.myreportlinks.com

▶**Stately Knowledge: Massachusetts**
At this Web site you will find facts and figures on the state of
Massachusetts including the state's capital, population, historical sites,
and additional Internet resources.

Link to this Internet site from http://www.myreportlinks.com

▶**Today in History**
At this Library of Congress Web site you will learn about Edgar Allan
Poe, a famous writer who was born in Boston, Massachusetts. Included
is a brief overview of some of his important works and his family life.

Link to this Internet site from http://www.myreportlinks.com

▶**U.S. Census Bureau: Massachusetts**
At this Web site you will find the official census statistics on the state
of Massachusetts. Learn about the population demographics, business
facts, geography facts, and more.

Link to this Internet site from http://www.myreportlinks.com

Capital
Boston

Land Area
7,838 square miles

Counties
14

Lowest Point
Sea level, Atlantic coast

Nicknames
Bay State, Old Bay State

Population
6,349,097*

Mammals
Cat: tabby
Dog: Boston terrier
Horse: Morgan
Marine animal: right whale

Bird
Chickadee

Fish
Cod

Flag
The state motto runs in a banner around a blue shield on a white background. On the blue shield is an American Indian holding a shield an an arrow pointing downward, which signifies peace.

Flower
Mayflower

Motto
Ense Petit Placidam Sub Libertate Quitem (By the sword we seek peace, but peace only under liberty)

Song
"All Hail Massachusetts"

Tree
Elm

Gained Statehood
February 6, 1788;
the sixth state.

*Population reflects the 2000 census.

In the First Place

Massachusetts is named for an American Indian tribe that once lived south of modern-day Boston in an area known as Great Blue Hill. They were called the *Massachusett*, meaning "near the great hill." Massachusetts is one of the original thirteen colonies and, in 1788, was the sixth to become a state. Yet, it is not officially called a state.

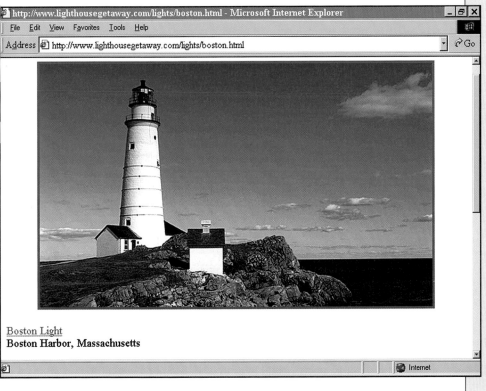

Boston Light
Boston Harbor, Massachusetts

▲ Built in 1716, Boston Light was America's first lighthouse. It is in Boston Harbor.

It is known as a Commonwealth. So are Kentucky, Pennsylvania, and Virginia. In the second draft of the Massachusetts constitution, ratified in 1780, John Adams used the word "commonwealth" for a body of people who make up a nation or state. This was a popular term to use in legal writings of the time.[1]

Massachusetts is small in size. It ranks forty-fourth of the fifty states in total area, with 10,554 square miles. Only Vermont, New Jersey, Connecticut, Hawaii, Delaware, and Rhode Island are smaller. Yet for its size, it has an amazing array of "firsts" in America. It is the site of the first English colonial Thanksgiving (Plymouth, 1621). Massachusetts boasts the first college (Harvard, 1636), the first state public school system (1647), the first major public library (Boston, 1854), the first basketball game (Springfield, 1891), and the first World Series baseball game (Boston, 1903), to name just a few.

Massachusetts may be small in size, but it is big in population. With nearly 6,400,000 people (based on the 2000 census), it is one of the most densely populated of the fifty states. Only twelve states have more people.

The Commonwealth of Massachusetts is part of New England, a six-state area located in the northeastern United States. Maine is the only New England state that does not border Massachusetts. Vermont and New Hampshire share its northern border, while Connecticut and Rhode Island lie to the south. The Atlantic Ocean lies to the east, and New York borders Massachusetts to the west. Massachusetts looks roughly like a rectangle on a map, with Cape Cod, an elbow-shaped piece of land, sticking out into the Atlantic.

Massachusetts is called the Bay State for the many bays of water along its eastern coast. Bay Staters are known for pride in their country, the Commonwealth, and themselves. They are especially proud of the role that Massachusetts played in colonial days and during the American Revolution. In fact, Massachusetts is sometimes called the birthplace of America.

▶ The Capital

The Boston area shows off Massachusetts at its historic best. Boston, founded in 1630, is the capital city. It is a seaport town on Massachusetts Bay located at the mouths of the Charles and Mystic rivers. The best way to see Boston is to walk. It is a big town—population of 589,141—that does not cover a large area.[2]

Boston covers only 46 square miles, and 25 percent of that is water. Here, modern living easily mingles with ghosts of colonial days. Visitors can walk the Freedom Trail. They follow this two-and-a-half-mile, red brick road

▲ Boston, the capital of Massachusetts, is New England's leading business, financial, government, and transportation center.

to centuries-old sites that tell the story of the first days of the American Revolution. There is a stop at the Old Granary Burying Ground, where Samuel Adams and John Hancock—both signers of the Declaration of Independence—are buried. A favorite site is the Old North Church. It was there, wrote poet Henry Wadsworth Longfellow, that Paul Revere was guided by lanterns—"one if by land, two if by sea"—to warn that the British were coming. Paul Revere's house is also on the Freedom Trail. Revere, a silversmith, is the folk hero of the American Revolution. His famous horseback ride, along with William Dawes and Samuel Prescott, on April 18, 1775, warned the people of the coming war.[3]

The Freedom Trail also leads to the USS *Constitution*, nicknamed *Old Ironsides*. Launched in 1797, it is the oldest commissioned ship in the U.S. Navy. It was restored between 1927 and 1931. The ship, which is open to the public, is permanently docked in Boston Harbor at the Charlestown Navy Yard.

Boston's main business is government, but it has other attractions, too. Faneuil Hall Marketplace (also called Quincy Market), an indoor-outdoor shopping mall, is always crowded with tourists. Merchant Peter Faneuil (1700–43) donated the building known as Faneuil Hall to the city on the condition that it remain a market and meeting place. Today the bottom level contains shops and restaurants, and the second floor is still used for public events.

Boston also boasts lovely old homes. In addition, other attractions are the renowned Boston Museum of Fine Arts, the New England Aquarium with its giant fish tank, and the world-famous Children's Museum with its many hands-on exhibits.

For those interested in sports, the Boston area is the place to be. Fenway Park is home to the Boston Red Sox baseball team. The 2001–02 National Football League champion New England Patriots play at nearby Foxboro Stadium. The well-known basketball dynasty, the Boston Celtics, and Boston's ice hockey team, the Bruins, both play at the FleetCenter.

Greater Boston Area

Of course, there are college sports, too. The greater Boston area contains fifty colleges and universities. Two of the world's most famous and respected institutions are located just across the Charles River in Cambridge. Harvard

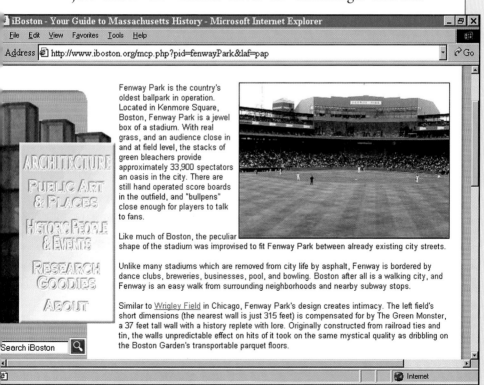

iBoston - Your Guide to Massachusetts History - Microsoft Internet Explorer

File   Edit   View   Favorites   Tools   Help

Address http://www.iboston.org/mcp.php?pid=fenwayPark&laf=pap   Go

ARCHITECTURE

PUBLIC ART & PLACES

HISTORIC PEOPLE & EVENTS

RESEARCH GOODIES

ABOUT

Search iBoston

Fenway Park is the country's oldest ballpark in operation. Located in Kenmore Square, Boston, Fenway Park is a jewel box of a stadium. With real grass, and an audience close in and at field level, the stacks of green bleachers provide approximately 33,900 spectators an oasis in the city. There are still hand operated score boards in the outfield, and "bullpens" close enough for players to talk to fans.

Like much of Boston, the peculiar shape of the stadium was improvised to fit Fenway Park between already existing city streets.

Unlike many stadiums which are removed from city life by asphalt, Fenway is bordered by dance clubs, breweries, businesses, pool, and bowling. Boston after all is a walking city, and Fenway is an easy walk from surrounding neighborhoods and nearby subway stops.

Similar to Wrigley Field in Chicago, Fenway Park's design creates intimacy. The left field's short dimensions (the nearest wall is just 315 feet) is compensated for by The Green Monster, a 37 feet tall wall with a history replete with lore. Originally constructed from railroad ties and tin, the walls unpredictable effect on hits of it took on the same mystical quality as dribbling on the Boston Garden's transportable parquet floors.

Internet

▲ Fenway Park is home to the Boston Red Sox. It opened on April 20, 1912, making it America's oldest ballpark in operation.

University started as a one-teacher school in New Towne (later renamed Cambridge). It was named for a Puritan minister, John Harvard, who donated his books and half his estate to the new school. Massachusetts Institute of Technology (M.I.T.) dates from 1865. It is an outstanding institution of scientific learning and research.

The city of Cambridge has its history, too. On Brattle Street is the Longfellow National Historic Site. George Washington set up his Revolutionary War headquarters during 1775 and 1776 in this grand mansion. It was later the home of Henry Wadsworth Longfellow, who lived there for forty-five years.

▶ North of Boston

North of Boston is the splendidly scary town of Salem. The Salem area was awash in witch hysteria in 1692. Three museums—the Salem Witch Museum, the Witch Dungeon Museum, and the Salem Witch Village—are dedicated to this time period. At the time, a series of investigations and persecutions resulted in the execution of nineteen so-called "witches" and the imprisonment of many others. It all started when a doctor named William Griggs said that several Salem Village girls had broken out into fits, because they were victims of witchcraft. The girls accused three women—Sarah Osburn, Sarah Good, and a West Indian slave named Tituba (pronounced *Tit-chew-ba*)—of telling them voodoo tales.[4]

In addition, Salem was an important nineteenth-century seaport. Visitors can view its seafaring past at the Peabody Essex Museum. Also located north of Boston are Lexington and Concord. The American Revolution began in Lexington when the first shots were fired on April 19,

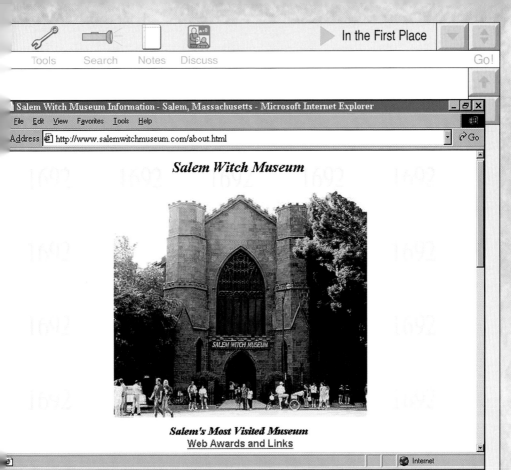

Salem Witch Museum Information - Salem, Massachusetts - Microsoft Internet Explorer

File   Edit   View   Favorites   Tools   Help

Address 🔲 http://www.salemwitchmuseum.com/about.html   🔗 Go

Salem Witch Museum

Salem's Most Visited Museum
Web Awards and Links

Internet

▲ *In 1692, nineteen people accused of being witches were hanged for their alleged crimes. Although these claims later proved false, the history of the Salem Witch Trials interests many people today.*

1775. Every year, people dressed as colonial Patriots and British Redcoats meet to reenact the famous fight.

Concord was also the home of essayist and poet Henry David Thoreau (1817–62). In 1845, Thoreau built a cabin near Walden Pond, about two miles south of Concord. His book, *Walden* (also called *Life in the Woods*) was written in 1854. Walden describes his simple life there over a two-year period. Another famous author, Louisa May Alcott, grew up in Concord and Boston. She is known for her novel *Little Women,* the story of four sisters growing up in New England in the 1800s.

Farther northwest, in the Merrimack Valley, is another historic site. During the Industrial Revolution of the 1700s and early 1800s, America began to rely on products made by large manufacturers instead of artisans working in small shops. On the banks of the Merrimack River is Lowell, which was once an entire city of cotton-textile mills. It is named for Francis Cabot Lowell, who built the first cotton mill in Massachusetts in 1814. Mills in Lowell and other cities, such as Fall River and Lynn, brought manufacturing to the state and improved the economy. The mills were also some of the first factories to hire large amounts of women. These "mill girls" worked for an average of three years before moving on. The textile industry in Lowell is now gone, but the buildings are reminders of its past.

One of Lowell's best-known residents is writer Jack Kerouac, who is famous for his novel *On the Road*. It is also the birthplace of artist James McNeill Whistler. His most famous work is *Arrangement in Grey and Black, No. 1: The Artist's Mother*, but most people know it simply as *Whistler's Mother*.

▶ Famous Bay Staters

Massachusetts has many other famous native sons and daughters. Writers Emily Dickinson, Edgar Allan Poe, and Theodore Geisel (known as Dr. Seuss) came from the Bay State. So did inventors Eli Whitney (the cotton gin, 1794), Samuel Morse (the telegraph, 1844), and Elias Howe (the sewing machine, 1845). Massachusetts is also the birth-place of television late night hosts Jay Leno and Conan O'Brien, as well as film stars Geena Davis, Matt Damon, and Ben Affleck.

Many stars of the stage and screen perform during the year in western Massachusetts. This area in the Berkshire

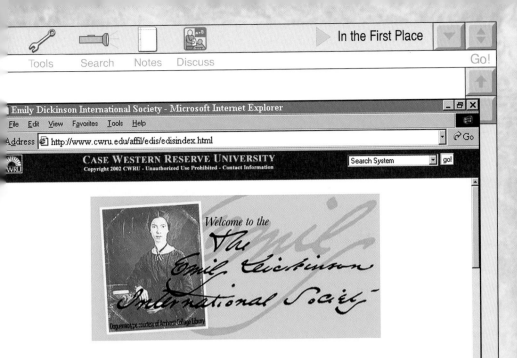

Welcome to the *The Emily Dickinson International Society*

Daguerreotype courtesy of Amherst College Library

2002 Pollak Scholar in Amherst Award

For the second year, The Emily Dickinson International Society will provide support for research on Emily Dickinson at institutions such as the Frost Library of Amherst College, the Jones Public Library, the Mount Holyoke College Archives, the Dickinson Homestead, the Evergreens, and the Amherst Historical Society.

For 2002, the $2,000 fellowship is named in honor of the second president of EDIS, Vivian Pollak, and is funded partially

▲ Emily Dickinson is considered one America's finest poets. Her seclusion from society and puzzling poetic verses have intrigued her readers to this day.

Hills calls itself America's premier cultural resort. Tanglewood is the summer home of the Boston Symphony Orchestra, founded in 1881. The oldest dance celebration in the country is the Jacob's Pillow Dance Festival in Becket. Every summer, top stars perform at the Williamstown and Berkshire Theatre Festivals, as well as Shakespeare & Company in Lenox. Stockbridge has the Norman Rockwell Museum, which has the largest collection of original paintings by this American artist. Pittsfield has Arrowhead, the estate where Herman Melville wrote *Moby Dick*. Amherst is the birthplace of Emily Dickinson,

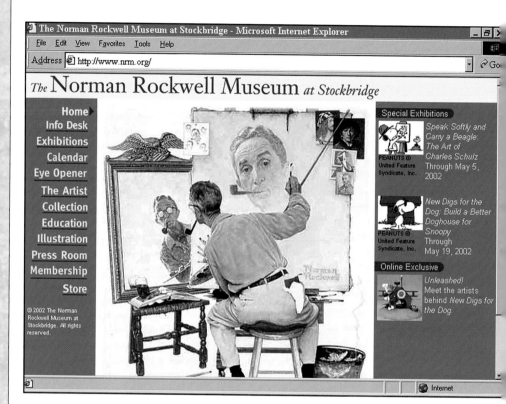

File Edit View Favorites Tools Help

Address 🔗 http://www.nrm.org/

The *Norman Rockwell Museum* at *Stockbridge*

Home
Info Desk
Exhibitions
Calendar
Eye Opener
The Artist
Collection
Education
Illustration
Press Room
Membership
Store

Special Exhibitions

PEANUTS ® United Feature Syndicate, Inc.
Speak Softly and Carry a Beagle: The Art of Charles Schulz Through May 5, 2002

PEANUTS ® United Feature Syndicate, Inc.
New Digs for the Dog: Build a Better Doghouse for Snoopy Through May 19, 2002

Online Exclusive
Unleashed! Meet the artists behind *New Digs for the Dog.*

Internet

▲ *The Norman Rockwell Museum, located in Stockbridge, holds the largest collection of the artist's original paintings.*

and the site of the University of Massachusetts, as well as Amherst and Hampshire colleges. Springfield is home to the Naismith Memorial Basketball Hall of Fame. The sport was created by Dr. James Naismith in 1891 as a cold-weather activity. The Volleyball Hall of Fame is located in Holyoke.

From the great beaches of the Atlantic coast to the music-filled Berkshire Hills, Massachusetts has much to offer its residents and visitors.

Land and Climate

About 28 million people visit Massachusetts each year. Most of them go to Boston, the most populous city in New England, or Cape Cod, one of the nation's most famous seashore resorts. Both are in the eastern part of the state, in the hard, flat region known as the coastal lowland.

▶ Out on the Cape

Thousands of years ago, glaciers carved out the indented coast of Massachusetts. Elbow-shaped Cape Cod juts sixty-five miles out into the Atlantic Ocean, with 500 miles of shoreline. On the Cape is Hyannis, a seaside resort and summer home of the late President John F. Kennedy and the Kennedy family. At the bend of the elbow-shaped land is the town of Chatham with its more than hundred-year-old lighthouse. Out at the tip of the cape is Provincetown, a haven for artists, those in the fishing industry, and tourists.

Nantucket Sound, south of Cape Cod, is dotted with many islands. The largest and most visited islands on the Cape are Nantucket and Martha's Vineyard. Nantucket has nineteenth-century charm. About eight hundred houses and buildings that were built before 1850 still stand on the islands. Automobiles are discouraged—bicycles are the preferred mode of transportation. Martha's Vineyard is larger and closer to the mainland. It was discovered by explorer Bartholomew Gosnold. He called it a vineyard because of the wild grapes that grew there, and named it after his baby daughter, Martha.[1]

▲ *Cape Cod is an elbow-shaped peninsula on the coast of Massachusetts. During the summer months, visitors flock to the islands of Martha's Vineyard and Nantucket, located just south of the Cape.*

▶ South of Boston

The city of Boston is nearly in the middle of this coastal lowland area. South of Boston is the indented coast, which was formed by great glaciers of ice that carved out the land thousands of years ago. Located here is Plymouth Rock, the site where Pilgrims first stepped onto North America after sixty-six days on the *Mayflower*. A replica called the *Mayflower II* is located nearby. Plimoth Plantation recreates the 1627 Plymouth community with a living history museum. There is also history of another kind here at New Bedford. At the New Bedford Whaling Museum, tourists take a tour through the whaling industry in America. The Seamen's Bethel, a chapel in New Bedford, is noted in the most famous of all whale stories, *Moby Dick* by Herman Melville.

The Heartland

Central Massachusetts is the heartland of the Commonwealth. It is a region of rolling plains, elevations of up to 1,000 feet, and many streams. Quabin Reservoir, the state's largest body of water, is in central Massachusetts. So are dairy farms and meadows, along with the pine and birch trees that grow in abundance. Worcester, the second-largest city in New England, is also located here.

South of Worcester is Old Sturbridge Village, which recreates a rural New England community of the 1830s. The staff, dressed in period clothing, go about daily chores in forty restored homes and craft shops.

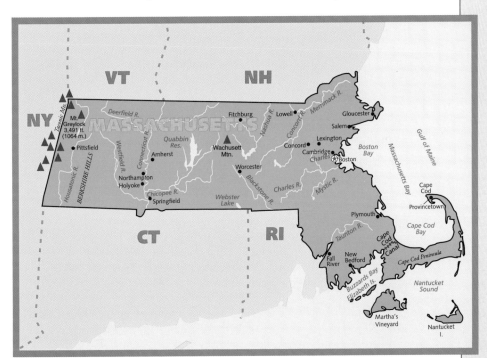

▲ A map of Massachusetts.

Wachusett Mountain, north of Worcester, is a popular southern New England ski area. The western part of this area slopes down to the fertile land along the banks of the Connecticut River. This is the state's most important agricultural region.

To the West

Western Massachusetts, stretching from the Connecticut River valley to the border with New York State, has the Berkshire Hills and the Taconic Mountains. Mount Greylock, the Bay State's highest point at 3,491 feet, is in the Berkshires. The Housatonic River also flows through this area.

The Great Outdoors

Massachusetts has a temperate climate typical of the New England states. Temperatures range from an average of 26°F in January to about 71°F in July. Summers are usually warm and humid. Annual rainfall ranges from about 42 inches on the coast to 45 inches in the west. The weather can be very different in the east and west. With mild ocean winds blowing inland in winter, Provincetown on the tip of Cape Cod is generally warmer and drier than Pittsfield on the western border. The west gets the biggest snow-storms—up to 75 inches a year. The coolest place to be is in the upland region of central Massachusetts.

The Bay State is a great place to walk along the beach or tour historic sites. It is equally pleasing to those who just enjoy being outdoors. There are nineteen main river systems: the best known are the Charles, Connecticut, and Merrimack rivers. Unfortunately, despite cleanup efforts, many of the rivers and lakes are not good for swimming. This is especially true of the meandering

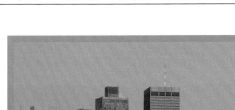

▲ *The Charles River divides the cities of Boston and Cambridge. It is a popular place for canoeists and rowing crews.*

Charles River, which separates Boston from Cambridge. Still, it is a favorite site for college rowing crews and people that canoe for fun.

In addition to its dense population and large amount of businesses, Massachusetts has about 150 state forests, parks, and reservations, including three national wildlife refuges. Not far from downtown Boston is the Arnold Arboretum, which has one of the largest collections of trees and shrubs in the United States. To add to these attractions, Massachusetts has a body of water with what may be the longest name in the entire country. It is Lake Chargoggagoggmanchauggagoggchaubunagungamaugg. Translated from the language of the Nipmuc Indians, it means "You fish on your side; I fish on my side; nobody fishes in the middle!"[2]

Chapter 3

Bay Stater Business

The number one business in Massachusetts is the service industry. The majority of people work at providing services for others, rather than making a product. This includes the computer software industry, health care, engineering companies, education, finance, real estate, and banking. Massachusetts General Hospital is a leading center for medical research. Fleet Bank, based in Boston, is one of the largest banking companies in the United States.

Tourism is also a big service industry for the state. More than 26 million tourists spend time in the

▲ *Located in Salem, the House of the Seven Gables, the birthplace and home of author Nathaniel Hawthorne, is the oldest surviving mansion in New England. This mansion was Hawthorne's inspiration for writing his 1851 novel* The House of the Seven Gables. *It is now a tourist attraction in Massachusetts.*

Commonwealth each year. Many of them flock to the beaches of Cape Cod or the offshore islands. Millions also visit Boston, Plymouth, and Salem.

Manufacturing

Manufacturing accounts for about 18 percent of the Commonwealth's employment. Manufacturing became popular in the 1640s when John Winthrop, Jr., opened a saltworks in Beverly. A saltworks is a place where salt is prepared to be sold to the public. However, it was Francis Cabot Lowell who really gave manufacturing a boost. After studying textile operations in England, he opened a mill in Waltham in 1814. His associates developed the city of Lowell along the Merrimack River into a textile manufacturing giant of the times. Not long afterward, Massachusetts became known for its shoe factories, as well. Today, the Commonwealth is a chief maker of electronic equipment, industrial machinery, metal products, and printing and publishing equipment. The first printing press was set up in Cambridge in 1638.

Commercial Fishing

Massachusetts has long been a region of commercial fishing, even though it now makes up only about one percent of the economy. The chief fishing ports are Boston, Falls River, New Bedford, Salem, Gloucester, Provincetown, and Plymouth. About half of the scallops in the United States are harvested in New Bedford, but the nearby areas are also rich in flounder, cod, clams, crabs, and other seafood.

Fishing was at its height in Massachusetts at the beginning of the twentieth century, when quick transportation allowed fresh fish to be shipped for long distances in a

▲ At the beginning of the twentieth century, commercial fishing in Massachusetts was an important part of the state's economy.

short time. Fishing has fallen on hard times, however. Overfishing in the North Atlantic has depleted the supply of fish. The very technology that helps fishers bring in such good catches is also taking its toll on the fish population. As fish become more scarce, the fishing industry tries to come up with new technology to catch the already short supply.

▶ Agriculture

Massachusetts is an agricultural state, although not on a grand scale. The soil of the Commonwealth is too rocky and thin to produce great farms. Yet there are many small farms that cover about 14 percent of the land. They mainly produce cranberries, flowers, and shrubs. Every year, Massachusetts is among the leaders in the nation in the overall production of cranberries. The Wampanoag natives, who mixed cranberries with deer meat to produce what they called *pemmican,* introduced the fruit to the Pilgrims. Massachusetts farms also grow corn and apples and produce maple syrup.

▶ Education

Massachusetts is noted for education. Half of all the Nobel Prize winners in the United States have come from colleges and universities within the Commonwealth.[1] In 1647, Massachusetts declared that any town of fifty or more people had to collect taxes for a school. The first public high school, English High School, was established in 1821. In 1852, Massachusetts became the first state to require children to attend school.

The Commonwealth has more than 120 colleges and universities. About fifty of these are in or around greater Boston, including Boston College, Boston University, Brandeis University, M.I.T., and Tufts University. Aside from Harvard, Massachusetts is home to Northeastern, the nation's largest private university. The first college for women, Wheaton College is located in nearby Norton. Another school, founded in 1837, Mount Holyoke is a member of the "Seven Sisters" of prestigious women's colleges. The others are Radcliffe, Smith, and Wellesley in Massachusetts; Barnard and Vassar in New York; and Bryn Mawr in Pennsylvania. However, since some of these colleges now admit men, the phrase "Seven Sisters" is rarely used.

Cambridge is home to Harvard, America's first school of higher learning.

Massachusetts boasts two of the world's finest research facilities for the study of the oceans. They are the Woods Hole Marine Biological Laboratory (founded in 1888) and the Woods Hole Oceanographic Institution (established in 1930), both located on Cape Cod.

The People of the Commonwealth

Hundreds of years ago, thousands of American Indians roamed the land that became Massachusetts. Soon after

Europeans began to explore North America, the native people began to die of diseases brought from across the ocean. Today, American Indians mainly live in the Cape Cod area, and make up about 2 percent of the state population. However, the American Indians' mark on Massachusetts history always remains because of names such as Narragansett, Nantucket, and Massachusetts itself.

Approximately 84 percent of the population is white and of European ancestry. There is a large Irish population in and around Boston. Irish immigrants began coming to Massachusetts in the 1840s in search of jobs. Many Italians live in Boston's North End, and there is a growing Hispanic-American population in the city, as well. A Greek community thrives in Lowell, and there is a large population of Portuguese Americans in the small town of New Bedford. Each year the Portuguese celebrate the Feast of the Blessed Sacrament, attracting thousands of people who come for the music and food.

African Americans make up little more than 5 percent of the population. Asian Americans are somewhat fewer, although a large Vietnamese community has sprung up in Lawrence.

▶ Religion in the Commonwealth

When the Puritans founded the Massachusetts Bay colony in the early 1600s, they finally had a place to freely practice their religion. Strangely enough, even though they fled Europe because of religious intolerance, they were very intolerant to anyone who would question the basic beliefs of their own faith. An example is the story of Anne Hutchinson (1591–1643). She migrated to Massachusetts with her husband in 1634 and began to organize weekly religious meetings. She criticized the Puritans for their

▲ *The Puritans arrived at Plymouth Rock in 1620 aboard the* Mayflower. *Pictured here is a replica of the ship built in 1957 by England as a gift to the United States.*

narrow concept of morality. For that she was tried, convicted, and thrown out of the colony. She and her husband went to Aquidneck, now part of Rhode Island.

Today little more than half of all citizens of the Commonwealth are Roman Catholic. There is a small Jewish community in Boston. Most of the other residents belong to the Episcopalian Church or the United Church of Christ.

Government

Government has been at work for a long time in Massachusetts. When the cornerstone was put in place for the New State House on July 4, 1795, Governor Samuel Adams said, "May the principles of our excellent Constitution, founded in Nature and in the Rights of Man, be ably defended here: And may the same principles be deeply engraven in the hearts of all citizens."[1]

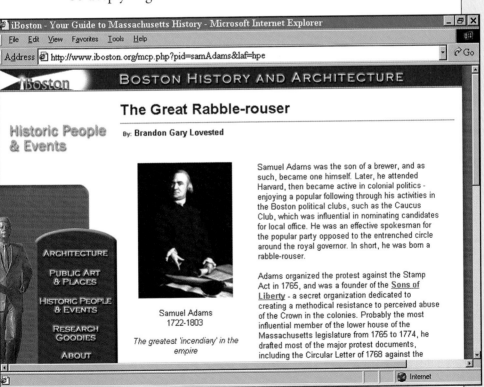

iBoston - Your Guide to Massachusetts History - Microsoft Internet Explorer   _ ♐ X

File   Edit   View   Favorites   Tools   Help

Address http://www.iboston.org/mcp.php?pid=samAdams&laf=hpe   ⌐ Go

iBoston   BOSTON HISTORY AND ARCHITECTURE

The Great Rabble-rouser

Historic People
& Events   By: Brandon Gary Lovested

Samuel Adams was the son of a brewer, and as such, became one himself. Later, he attended Harvard, then became active in colonial politics - enjoying a popular following through his activities in the Boston political clubs, such as the Caucus Club, which was influential in nominating candidates for local office. He was an effective spokesman for the popular party opposed to the entrenched circle around the royal governor. In short, he was born a rabble-rouser.

Adams organized the protest against the Stamp Act in 1765, and was a founder of the Sons of Liberty - a secret organization dedicated to creating a methodical resistance to perceived abuse of the Crown in the colonies. Probably the most influential member of the lower house of the Massachusetts legislature from 1765 to 1774, he drafted most of the major protest documents, including the Circular Letter of 1768 against the

ARCHITECTURE

PUBLIC ART
& PLACES

HISTORIC PEOPLE
& EVENTS

RESEARCH
GOODIES

ABOUT

Samuel Adams
1722-1803

The greatest 'incendiary' in the empire

                                              🌐 Internet

▲ *Samuel Adams was an American patriot and politician who founded the Sons of Liberty. He was the principal organizer of the Boston Tea Party.*

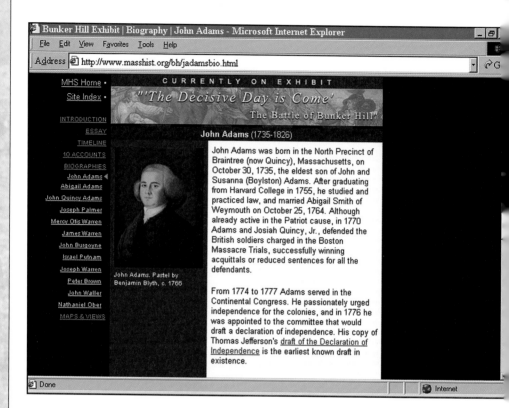

File Edit View Favorites Tools Help

Address http://www.masshist.org/bh/jadamsbio.html

MHS Home •
Site Index •

INTRODUCTION
ESSAY
TIMELINE
10 ACCOUNTS
BIOGRAPHIES
John Adams ◄
Abigail Adams
John Quincy Adams
Joseph Palmer
Mercy Otis Warren
James Warren
John Burgoyne
Israel Putnam
Joseph Warren
Peter Brown
John Waller
Nathaniel Ober
MAPS & VIEWS

CURRENTLY ON EXHIBIT

"'The Decisive Day is Come'
The Battle of Bunker Hill"

John Adams (1735-1826)

John Adams was born in the North Precinct of Braintree (now Quincy), Massachusetts, on October 30, 1735, the eldest son of John and Susanna (Boylston) Adams. After graduating from Harvard College in 1755, he studied and practiced law, and married Abigail Smith of Weymouth on October 25, 1764. Although already active in the Patriot cause, in 1770 Adams and Josiah Quincy, Jr., defended the British soldiers charged in the Boston Massacre Trials, successfully winning acquittals or reduced sentences for all the defendants.

From 1774 to 1777 Adams served in the Continental Congress. He passionately urged independence for the colonies, and in 1776 he was appointed to the committee that would draft a declaration of independence. His copy of Thomas Jefferson's draft of the Declaration of Independence is the earliest known draft in existence.

John Adams. Pastel by Benjamin Blyth, c. 1766

Done   Internet

John Adams served as the second president of the United States.

Since then, Massachusetts has sent four men to the White House. The second president of the United States, John Adams (served 1797–1801), was born in Quincy, where he is buried. He also served as the nation's first vice president and was a member of the Second Continental Congress that declared independence in 1776. His son, John Quincy Adams, was the sixth president (served 1825–29). He was also born and buried in Quincy. John F. Kennedy (served 1961–63), the thirty-fifth president, was born in Brookline. He was assassinated in Dallas, Texas, in 1963. He is buried in Arlington National Cemetery, Virginia. The forty-first

president, George Herbert Walker Bush (served 1989–93), was born in Milton.

Today, Massachusetts has twelve representatives in the federal government. It has ten members in the U.S. House of Representatives, and, as with every state, Massachusetts also elects two members to the U.S. Senate.

John Adams himself was the principal author of the Massachusetts Constitution, which was ratified in 1780. Many of its features were included in the federal Constitution, as well. Today, Massachusetts is the only one of the original thirteen states still governed by its first democratic constitution—the oldest such governing document in the world.

▶ The Executive Branch

The Massachusetts government is headed by a governor, who is elected for a four-year term. In addition to appointing department heads and nominating judges, the governor prepares the annual budget and has the power of veto, which means that he or she can reject laws passed by the legislature.

If the governor leaves or is removed from office for any reason, the lieutenant governor takes over. Other Commonwealth officials are the attorney general, who is the Commonwealth's head lawyer; the secretary of state, in charge of commonwealth records; the treasurer, custodian of all commonwealth funds; and the auditor, who sees that finances are in order. They all serve four-year terms.

The lieutenant governor and eight citizens elected by region for two-year terms form the executive council. They approve or disapprove the governor's appointments for different positions and certify election results.

The Legislative Branch

The legislative branch in Massachusetts is called the general court. It has a 40-member senate and a 160-member house of representatives. They all serve two-year terms. Added to the usual work of passing laws is a unique feature: Any citizen of Massachusetts can submit a bill to the general court. This is called the right of free petition. To become law, all bills, no matter where they originate, must be agreed upon by both houses and then sent to the governor. The governor then signs it and sends it back with recommended changes, vetos it, or does nothing. If the bill is vetoed, or turned down, by the governor, the general court can override the veto by a two-thirds vote in both houses. If the governor does nothing, the bill will become law in ten days. If the legislature's year ends during those ten days, the bill is called a pocket veto, and will not become a law.

The Judicial Branch

The Commonwealth's highest court is the Supreme Judicial Court of Massachusetts, which dates from 1692. It is the oldest continuously-operating court in the United States. Led by a chief justice and six associates, the court advises the other branches of government on questions of law. All judges in Massachusetts may serve until the age of seventy.

Local Government

Cities and towns throughout the Commonwealth are generally governed by mayors and city councils or a governing body known as a board of selectmen or aldermen. Their terms are usually one or two years.

A cherished tradition in Massachusetts government is

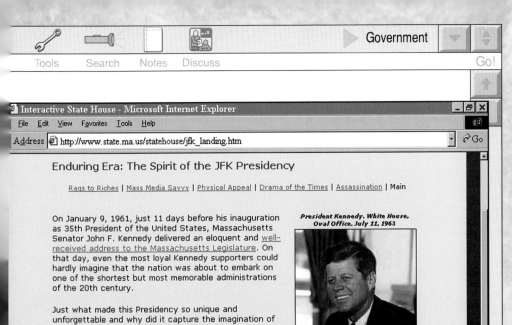

Interactive State House - Microsoft Internet Explorer

File   Edit   View   Favorites   Tools   Help

Address http://www.state.ma.us/statehouse/jfk_landing.htm   Go

Enduring Era: The Spirit of the JFK Presidency

Rags to Riches | Mass Media Savvy | Physical Appeal | Drama of the Times | Assassination | Main

On January 9, 1961, just 11 days before his inauguration as 35th President of the United States, Massachusetts Senator John F. Kennedy delivered an eloquent and well-received address to the Massachusetts Legislature. On that day, even the most loyal Kennedy supporters could hardly imagine that the nation was about to embark on one of the shortest but most memorable administrations of the 20th century.

Just what made this Presidency so unique and unforgettable and why did it capture the imagination of generations of Americans? For many born after President Kennedy's death, it's a difficult question to answer.

President Kennedy. White House, Oval Office. July 11, 1963

Photo: Cecil Stoughton, White House/ John F. Kennedy Library.

- Other presidents led the U.S. through difficult and prolonged wars.
- Many were more successful enacting groundbreaking legislation.
- Others were more skilled in diplomacy.

No single answer seems to answer the question. But it is easier to understand by considering the powerful combination of these five aspects to the man and his era.

Internet

▲ *The Kennedy family has had a major influence on the political life of Massachusetts. While serving as president, John F. Kennedy was assassinated in 1963.*

the old New England town meeting. Each spring, local voters get together in the town hall or auditorium to voice opinions and, sometimes, make decisions about their local government. Such gatherings can become quite spirited, as citizens debate about important local issues.

▶ The Kennedys

As a family, the Kennedys, of Hyannisport, have made their mark on the history of Massachusetts politics. The nine children of Joseph P. Kennedy, a controversial businessman and diplomat, and his wife, Rose Fitzgerald

Kennedy, have been part of Commonwealth life since the middle of the twentieth century. Their eldest son, Joseph, Jr., was killed in World War II. The next oldest, John F. Kennedy, was elected president in 1960. He was one of the more popular presidents to hold office. At his inauguration on a bitterly cold day the following January, he said, ". . . the torch has been passed to a new generation of Americans."[2] Sadly, he was assassinated in 1963. His brother, Robert, was also assassinated while campaigning for the presidency in 1968. Edward, the youngest son, is a long-standing member of the United States Senate.

New generations of Kennedys now serve in state and federal government posts. They continue this long-held tradition of public service, surviving personal scandal and continuing tragedy. In 1999, the former president's son, John F. Kennedy, Jr., was killed while piloting a plane on a trip from New Jersey to Massachusetts.

History: High Seas to High Tech

The story is repeated in classrooms all over the country. It tells how the Pilgrims braved the high seas of the Atlantic Ocean to land on Plymouth Rock in December 1620. This small group of 102 had first landed at Cape Cod after a sixty-six-day journey from Great Britain aboard the *Mayflower*. They thought that the soil was too poor to farm, and fresh water was scarce, so they sailed across Cape Cod Bay and stepped ashore at Plymouth.[1]

▲ *This painting,* Pilgrims Going to Church, *by George H. Boughton, depicts what life may have been like in the Plymouth Colony.*

▶ The First Settlers

The Pilgrims were not the the first to see the rugged New England coast. Native Indians had wandered this land for at least 3,500 years. It is thought that Leif Eriksson and his Norsemen explored the Cape Cod area around A.D. 1003. French explorer Samuel de Champlain made a map of the region in 1605, prior to the Pilgrims' arrival. Nine years later, Captain John Smith of the Virginia Colony drew a map of New England from Cape Cod to what is now the state of Maine.

The Pilgrim settlement, called the Plymouth or Old Colony, lived peacefully with American Indians during the early years. That was mainly because of their peace treaty with Massasoit, chief of the Wampanoag. In fact, the colony would probably not have survived without the aid of the Wampanoag. To celebrate the harvest, the Pilgrims invited the Wampanoag to a feast in November 1621. That feast has become the basis for the Thanksgiving holiday.

About twenty years later, the Plymouth Colony had grown to about three thousand people. They were no longer the only English settlement in the area. To the north, the Puritans had settled the Massachusetts Bay Company in 1630. By the 1640s, it had grown to over twenty thousand people. The Puritans, like the Pilgrims, had come to America for religious freedom. They were a fiercely independent lot and even minted their own money. This rebellious streak so annoyed England's King Charles I that he revoked their colony charter in 1684. When King William and Queen Mary took the English throne, they granted a new charter in 1691. It included not only the Puritans' land, but Plymouth, the islands of Nantucket and Martha's Vineyard, and Maine. The

Paul Revere rode from Charlestown to Lexington to warn Samuel Adams and John Hancock that the British were coming. In the background is the steeple of the Old North Church, where two lanterns were hung, signaling to the silversmith that the British were coming by sea and that he was to begin his ride.

boundaries stayed that way until Maine became a separate state in 1820.

Peace between the settlers and the Wampanoag ended with King Philip's War in 1675. Philip was Massasoit's son. Philip feared that the English were threatening his people's way of life. He was eventually captured and killed. Raids became common in southeastern and central Massachusetts. Even so, by 1765, the population of the Massachusetts colony had reached about 222,000.

Rebellion in the Colony

The city of Boston became a hotbed of unrest in the years leading to the American Revolution. There were now thirteen English colonies in America spread along the Atlantic coast. Colonists were growing angrier over taxation laws and their lack of representation in the British Parliament. Cries for independence were raised.

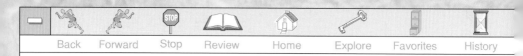

Massachusetts was thriving. Money was coming in from overseas trade and a growing shipbuilding industry. The colonists, though, were restless. As England continued to raise taxes, the colonists became increasingly angry. When England imposed the Stamp Act in 1765, taxing newspapers and most other printed materials, the colonists formed the Sons of Liberty in protest. They were outraged because they were being taxed when they had no representatives in England or votes in the British Parliament. Finally, when England placed a tax on tea in December 1773, the Sons of Liberty dressed as American Indians and dumped hundreds of tea chests into Boston Harbor. This act of rebellion, called the Boston Tea Party, infuriated the British.

In April 1775, the British, known as Redcoats for the color of their uniforms, headed toward the towns of Lexington and Concord, Massachusetts. The Revolutionary War had begun. One of its most famous battles was called the Battle of Bunker Hill, in Charlestown, now part of Boston, on June 17, 1775. Although the battle was named for Bunker Hill, it was actually fought on Breed's Hill. The British won the battle but lost 1,000 out of their original force of 2,500 soldiers. As a result, the Colonials gained great confidence.[2]

The Revolutionary War ended with the signing of a peace treaty in 1783. In 1788, Massachusetts became the sixth state to approve the new United States Constitution.

▶ The Nineteenth Century

The nineteenth century brought many immigrants, especially the Irish, to Massachusetts. The Commonwealth began to change from a rural state to an industrial one.

Boston nicely combines the ▷ *old with the new. Pictured here is Trinity Church (left), built between 1872 and 1877. On the right is the John Hancock building, built one hundred years later in 1976. Both have won awards for their outstanding architecture.*

The Civil War was fought from 1861 to 1865; mainly over the issues of slavery and states' rights. About 150,000 men from the Bay State fought for the Union, including several all-African-American regiments.

Massachusetts had a long history of antislavery views. It had abolished slavery back in 1780. Ex-slave Frederick Douglass, one of the greatest human rights leaders of the nineteenth century, worked with the Antislavery Society in Massachusetts in the early 1840s.[3] Another Massachusetts native, William Lloyd Garrison, founded an antislavery newspaper called *The Liberator*. The state also featured the Black Freedom Trail, a series of hiding places for slaves that were trying to reach freedom by means of the Underground Railroad.

Massachusetts was also home to one of the most famous army regiments of the Civil War. The Fifty-fourth Massachusetts Infantry was made up of free blacks from all over the state. Their actions included the storming of Confederate positions at Battery Wagner. Their exploits were depicted in the 1989 movie *Glory*, starring Matthew Broderick and Denzel Washington.[4]

By the end of the Civil War, Massachusetts had become one of the most densely populated states in the country. In the following years, the state continued to increase in population and the amount of goods manufactured. When the United States entered World War I, in 1917, Bay State factories supplied the United States military with equipment. After the war, however, the shoe and textile industries shifted to the South, where labor was cheaper. This, coupled with the Great Depression, left about half of the state's workers jobless.

World War II, which the United States entered in 1941, increased manufacturing. The government needed factories to produce goods that would help the war effort. Once again, the Bay State became a leading producer of wartime materials.

Since the 1950s, Massachusetts has become a region of high-tech industries, growing out of the development of computers and other technological advances. It continues to thrive in service industries such as banking, insurance, medical, and educational fields.

According to its citizens, Massachusetts is the first place a person would want to be.

Chapter Notes

Chapter 1. In the First Place

1. "Massachusetts Facts," *Citizen Information Service: William Francis Galvin, Secretary of the Commonwealth*, n.d., <http://www.state.ma.us/sec/cis/cismaf/mfla.htm> (August 6, 2002).

2. Borgna Brunner, ed., *Time Almanac 2002* (Boston: Family Education Company, 2001), p. 154.

3. Henry Wadsworth Longfellow, as posted, "Paul Revere's Ride," *The Paul Revere House,* 1860, 1997, <http://www.paulreverehouse.org/events/poem.html> (August 7, 2002).

4. Richard B. Trask, "Witch Hysteria," *The Danvers, Massachusetts Homepage*, n.d., <http://www.danvers-ma.org/witch.htm> (July 31, 2002).

Chapter 2. Land and Climate

1. "One-Minute Guide to Martha's Vineyard," *Martha's Vineyard Chamber of Commerce,* 1996–2002, <http://www.mvy.com/minute_guide.html> (August 6, 2002).

2. "History," Webster, *Dudley, Oxford Chamber of Commerce*, n.d., <http://www.wdo-chamber.com/history.htm> (August 7, 2002).

Chapter 3. Bay Stater Business

1. "Knowledge-Creation Infrastructure," *Massachusetts Department of Economic Development,* 2001, <http://www.massconnect.state.ma.us/showpage.asp?file=technolog/techinfrastructure.htm> (August 7, 2002).

Chapter 4. Government

1. Samuel Adams, quoted, "Massachusetts Facts: Part Three," *Citizen Information Service: William Francis Galvin, Secretary of the Commonwealth*, n.d., <http://www.state.ma.us/sec/cis/cismaf/mf3.htm> (August 7, 2002).

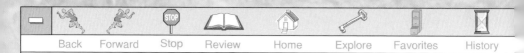

2. William A. DeGregorio, *The Complete Book of U.S. Presidents: From George Washington to Bill Clinton* (New York: Wings Books, 1997), p. 554.

Chapter 5. History: High Seas to High Tech

1. "The Mayflower Compact, 1620," *Pilgrim Hall Museum*, July 14, 1998, <http://www.pilgrimhall.org/compcon.htm> (August 6, 2002).

2. Allan R. Millett and Peter Maslowski, *For the Common Defense: A Military History of the United States of America* (New York: Free Press, 1994), p. 65.

3. Office of Affirmative Action/Equal Opportunity/Minority Affairs, "Frederick Douglass: Statesman, Publisher, Abolitionist, 1817–1895," *Bridgewater State College Hall of Black Achievement*, December 20, 2000, <http://www.bridgew.edu/HOBA/douglass.htm> (October 3, 2002).

4. Thomas R. Fasulo, "Fifty-fourth Massachusetts Infantry," *Battle of Olustee Homepage*, n.d., <extlab1.entnem.ufl.edu/olustee/54th_MS_inf.html> (July 19, 2002).

Further Reading

Barenblat, Rachel. *Massachusetts, the Bay State.* Milwaukee, Wis.: Stevens, Gareth Inc., 2002.

Erickson, Paul. *Daily Life in the Pilgrim Colony, 1636.* New York: Houghton Mifflin Company, 2001.

Feinstein, Stephen. *John Adams.* Berkeley Heights, N.J.: MyReportLinks.com Books, 2002.

Frisch, Aaron. *The History of the Boston Red Sox.* Mankato, Minn.: The Creative Company, 2002.

Joseph, Paul. *Massachusetts.* Minneapolis, Minn.: ABDO Publishing Company, 1998.

———. *The Boston Celtics.* Minneapolis, Minn.: ABDO Publishing Company, 1997.

Klingel, Cynthia Fitterer and Robert B. Noyed. *Paul Revere's Ride.* Chanhassen, Minn.: The Child's World, Inc., 2001.

McAuliffe, Emily. *Massachusetts.* Danbury, Conn.: Children's Press, 1998.

Roop, Connie and Peter Roop, eds. *Pilgrim Voices: Our First Year in the New World.* New York: Walker & Company, 1997.

Schultz, Randy. *John F. Kennedy.* Berkeley Heights, N.J.: MyReportLinks.com Books, 2002.

Thoreau, Henry David and Brooks Atkinson, ed. *Walden & Other Writings of Henry David Thoreau.* New York: Random House, Inc., 1992.

Index